SRA Art Connections

Level K

Authors

Rosalind Ragans, Ph.D., Senior Author

Willis Bing Davis
Tina Farrell
Jane Rhoades Hudak, Ph.D.
Gloria McCoy
Bunyan Morris
Nan Yoshida

Contributing Writer

Patricia Carter

The Music Center of Los Angeles County

SRA
McGraw-Hill

Columbus, Ohio

A Division of The McGraw-Hill Companies

Credits

13, Louvre, Paris; **26,** (Back, L to R) Kimo Kimura, Kenneth Bowman (Front) Kenneth B. Talley, John Pennington. Lewitzky Dance Company "Impressions #2" (Vincent van Gogh.) Photo: Vic Luke; **29,** Photograph © 1996 Detroit Institute of Arts, Dirk Bakker, Photographer; **31,** © 1998 Estate of Grant Wood/Licensed by VAGA, New York, NY, Courtesy of the Curtis Galleries Inc. Minneapolis, MN; **44,** AMAN Dance Company "Suite of Appalachian Music and Dance." Photo: Craig Schwartz; **47,** Photograph courtesy of Jerry Pinkney; **49,** UPI/CORBIS-BETTMAN; **62,** Paul Salamunovich. Photo: Robert Millard © 1993 Courtesy of the Los Angeles Master Chorale; **67,** Dominique Berretty/Black Star; **80,** May Day Parade & Festival. Photo: Courtesy of In the Heart of the Beast Puppet and Mask Theatre; **83,** Photograph Courtesy of Christopher Downs; **85,** Courtesy of the Museum of Fine Arts Boston; **98,** Geri Keams, Storyteller. Photo: Craig Schwartz, © 1990; **101,** Nelson-Atkins Museum of Art, Kansas City, including Shuttlecocks, 1994, by Coosje van Bruggen and Claes Oldenburg; **103,** Courtesy Maria Martinez, © Jerry Jacka Photography; **116,** Chic Street Man. Photo: Neil Rickle; **119,** Berte Morisot; **140,** *Yellow Horse*—© Douglas Mazonowicz/ Gallery of Prehistoric Art; **141,** *Tutankhamen Mask, side view*—Brian Brake, Photo Researchers; **142,** *Mona Lisa*—Louvre, Paris France, Erich Lessing, Art Resource, NY; **143,** *Susan Comforting the Baby*—Museum of Fine Arts, Houston, TX; The John A. and Audrey Jones Beck Collection; **148,** Aaron Haupt/Aaron Haupt Photography; **150,** Michael Newman/PhotoEdit; **152,** Mark Burnet.

SRA/McGraw-Hill

A Division of The McGraw·Hill Companies

Send all inquiries to:
SRA/McGraw-Hill
250 Old Wilson Bridge Road
Suite 310
Worthington, OH 43085

ISBN 0-02-688314-7

1 2 3 4 5 6 7 8 9 VHP 02 01 00 99 98 97

Authors

Senior Author
Rosalind Ragans, Ph.D.,
Associate Professor Emerita,
Georgia Southern University

Willis Bing Davis,
Head of Art Department,
Central State University, Ohio

Tina Farrell,
Associate Director of Visual and
Performing Arts, Clear Creek Independent
School District, Texas

Jane Rhoades Hudak, Ph.D.,
Professor of Art Teacher Education,
Georgia Southern University

Gloria McCoy,
K–12 Art Supervisor,
Spring Branch Independent
School District, Texas

Bunyan Morris,
Art Teacher,
Laboratory School,
Georgia Southern University

Nan Yoshida,
Former Art Supervisor,
Los Angeles Unified School
District, California

Contributors

ARTSOURCE Music, Dance, Theater Lessons
The Music Center of Los
Angeles County Education Division,
Los Angeles, California

More About Aesthetics
Richard W. Burrows,
Executive Director,
Institute for Arts Education,
San Diego, California

Safe Use of Art Materials
Mary Ann Boykin, Visiting Lecturer,
Art Education; Director, The Art School
for Children and Young Adults,
University of Houston-Clear Lake,
Houston, Texas

Museum Education
Marilyn JS Goodman, Director
of Education, Solomon R. Guggenheim
Museum, New York, New York

**National Museum of Women
in the Arts Collection**
National Museum of Women in the
Arts, Washington, DC

Contributing Writer

Patricia Carter
Assistant Professor of Art Education
Georgia Southern University

Reviewers

Mary Ann Boykin
Visiting Lecturer, Art Education;
Director, The Art School for Children
and Young Adults
University of Houston-Clear Lake
Houston, TX

Cynthia M. Coleman
Kindergarten Teacher
Normandie Avenue School
Los Angeles Unified School District
Los Angeles, CA

Judy Gong
Multi-age Classroom Teacher
Pacific Elementary School
Lincoln Unified School District
Stockton, CA

Lori Groendyke Knutti
Art Education
Harrison Street Elementary School
Big Walnut Elementary School
Sunbury, OH

Carol S. James
Kindergarten Teacher
Nitsch Elementary School
Klein Independent School District
Houston, TX

Steven R. Sinclair
Art Teacher
Big Country Elementary School
Southwest I.S.D.
San Antonio, TX

Student Activity Testers

Madeline Jobrack
Brady Wooldridge
Emily Haupt
Matthew Ford
Abby McMillian
Christopher Byorth

TABLE OF CONTENTS

Unit 1 Line

Unit 2 Shape

Unit 3 Color

Unit 4 Space and Form

Unit 5 Texture

Unit 6 Rhythm, Balance, and Unity

More About . . .

What Is Art?

Art is . . .

Painting

Winslow Homer. (American). *Snap the Whip.* 1872. Oil on canvas. 12 × 20 inches. Metropolitan Museum of Art, New York, New York.

Drawing

Ito Jakuchu. (Japanese). *Fukurojin, the God of Longevity and Wisdom.* c. 1790. Hanging scroll, ink and light colors on paper. $45\frac{5}{8} \times 22\frac{1}{4}$ inches. Courtesty of Kimbell Museum, Fort Worth, Texas.

Sculpture

Artist unknown. (West Africa, Benin Kingdom). *Bronze head for the Altars of the Obas.* Mid-sixteenth century. Bronze. Superstock/ Christies, London, England.

Architecture

Frank Lloyd Wright/Gwathimey Siegel and Associates. (American).*The Solomon R. Guggenheim Museum.* New York, New York.

Printmaking

Katsushika Hokusai. (Japanese). *The Great Wave Off Kanagawa.* 1831–33. Polychrome woodblock print. $10\frac{1}{8} \times 14\frac{15}{16}$ inches. Metropolitan Museum of Art, New York, New York.

Pottery

Artist unknown. Kiangsi Province (China). *Jar.* (Ming Dynasty). 1426–35. Porcelain painted in underglaze blue. 19 inches high. Metropolitan Museum of Art, New York, New York. Gift of Robert E. Todd, 1937.

Weaving

Artist unknown. (United States). *Appalachian Basket.* Twentieth century. Split oak. 12 × 12 inches. Hudak private collection.

Toy Making

Artist unknown. (Russia). *Russian Doll.* 1991. Wood with oil paint. 8 inches high. Hudak private collection. Photograph by ©Tom Amedis.

Art is created by people.

Art talks with . . .

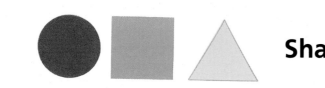

Line

Shape

Color

SPACE

FORM

TEXTURE

Rhythm

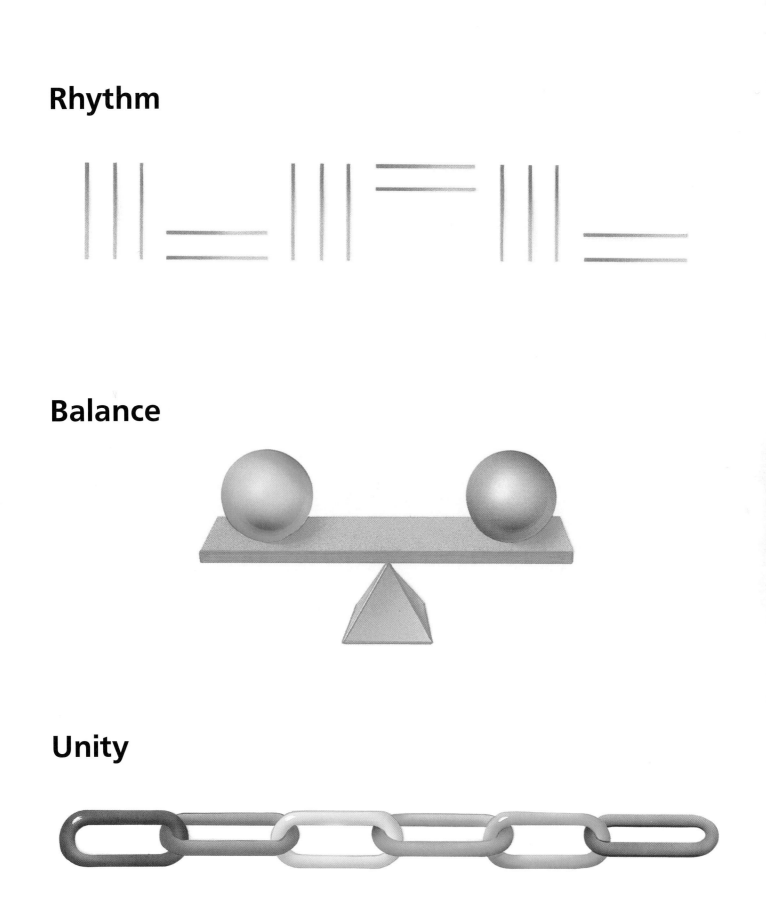

Balance

Unity

An Introduction to

Line

Katsushika Hokusai. (Japanese). *The Great Wave Off Kanagawa. 36 Views of Mount Fuji.* 1831–33. Polychrome woodblock print. $10\frac{1}{8} \times 14\frac{15}{16}$ inches. Metropolitan Museum of Art, New York, New York.

Artists use lines to create their artwork.

Can you find some different kinds of lines?

Artist **P**rofile

Katsushika Hokusai
1760–1849

Self-Portrait.

Katshusika Hokusai

- was a Japanese artist.
- created prints.
- made landscapes.

Thick and Thin Lines

Artist Unknown. Navajo (United States). *Classic Serape Style Wearing Blanket.* 1875. Plied cotton and Saxony wool. $73\frac{1}{2} \times 47$ inches. Utah Museum of Fine Arts, University of Utah, Salt Lake City, Utah.

Where do you see thick and thin lines in the picture?

Seeing like an artist

Find thick and thin lines on the walls and floor.

A **thick line** is wide.

A **thin line** is narrow.

Create

How would you use thick and thin lines to make a design?

Create a blanket for yourself with different lines.

Kristina Jimenez. Age 5. Tempera.

Different Kinds of Lines

W. H. Brown. (American). *Bareback Riders*. 1886. Oil on cardboard mounted on wood. $18\frac{1}{2} \times 24\frac{1}{4}$. National Gallery of Art, Washington, DC. Gift of Edgar William and Bernice Chrysler Garbisch. ©1996 Board of Trustees, National Gallery of Art, Washington, DC.

Find three different kinds of lines in the picture.

Seeing like an artist

Can you find straight, slanted, and curved lines around you?

Lines move in different directions.

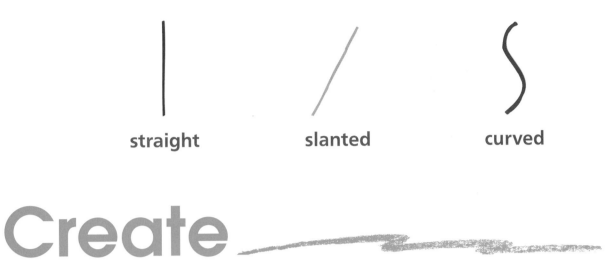

straight   slanted   curved

Create

What lines do you see at a circus?

Draw a circus picture with different lines.

Ashley Weber. Age 5. *Monkey's Fun Time.* Marker and paint.

Looking at *Smooth* and Rough Lines

Ito Jakuchu. (Japanese). *Fukurojin, the God of Longevity and Wisdom.* c 1790. Hanging Scroll, ink and light colors on paper. $45\frac{5}{8} \times 22\frac{1}{4}$ inches. Courtesy of the Kimbell Art Museum, Fort Worth, Texas.

Tell what things in the art would feel smooth or rough.

Look around the room. Find something that looks smooth.

Lines that show how things feel to the touch look different.

smooth   rough

Create

What does your favorite outdoor place look like?

Paint it using smooth and rough lines.

Madeline Jobrack. Age 5. *Me, a Turtle, and a Swingset.* Tempera.

Lines to Touch

Katsushika Hokusai. (Japanese). *Boy Juggling Shells.* Edo period. Album leaf, ink and color on paper. $13\frac{5}{16} \times 9\frac{1}{2}$ inches. Metropolitan Museum of Art, New York, New York. Charles Stewart Smith Collection. Gift of Mrs. Charles Stewart Smith, in memory of Charles Stewart Smith, 1914.

How would different parts in the picture feel if you could touch them?

Seeing like an artist

Trace lines in the air to show how your hair looks and feels.

Artists use **lines** to show how things feel.

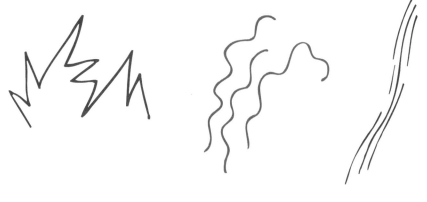

Create

How can you make lines that feel different?

Create a picture with lines you can touch.

Francisco Calixto. Age 5. *Los Colores.* Glue, chalk, and pastel.

Broken Lines

Artist Unknown. (Italy). *Ravenna Apse Mosaic (Detail).*
549 A.D. The Church of Saint Apollinaris, Ravenna, Italy.
Scala/Art Resource, New York.

Put your finger on a
broken line in this art.

**Seeing like
an artist**

Look at the
wall and floor.
Can you find
broken lines?

Lines with spaces between them
are **broken lines**.

● ● ● ● ● ●● ●

━━ ━━ ━━ ━ ━ ━━ ━

Create

How would you make a picture with spaces between lines?

Draw some animals with broken lines.

Jessica M. Hopkins. Age 5. *Horse.* Construction paper.

Lines Make Pictures

Winslow Homer. (American). *Snap the Whip.* 1872.
Oil on canvas. 12 × 20 inches. Metropolitan Museum of Art,
New York, New York. Gift of Christian A. Zabriskie, 1950.

What things in the picture look like they are moving?

Seeing like an artist

Trace in the air one thing that you see. What kinds of lines did you make?

Some **lines** show things standing still.

Some **lines** show things moving.

Create

How would you show yourself moving in a picture?

Draw yourself playing.

Tiffany Palmer. Age 5. *Playing Soccer.* Crayon.

Lines in Dance

Lewitzky Dance Company: Dancers in positions from "Impressions #2," a suite of dances choreographed by Bella Lewitzky, based on the painting "Starry Night" by Vincent van Gogh. (Back L to R) Kimo Kimura, Kenneth Bowman; (Front) Kenneth B. Talley, John Pennington.

Bella Lewitzky creates dances. Her dancers make curved, straight, and slanted lines with their bodies.

What To Do

Make lines with your body.

1. Look at the painting.
Name the kinds of lines
you see.

2. Move your body
to show each kind
of line.

Vincent van Gogh. (Dutch). *The Starry Night.* 1889.
Oil on canvas. $28\frac{3}{4} \times 36\frac{1}{2}$ inches. Museum of Modern Art.
New York, New York.

Extra Credit ·

Use your body to make a moon or a star.

Line

Reviewing Main Ideas

There are many kinds of lines.

You have seen and used different kinds of lines.

Hughie Lee-Smith. *The Piper*. 1953. Oil on composition board. 55.9 × 89.5 cm. Photograph © The Detroit Institute of Arts, Detroit, Michigan. Gift of Mr. and Mrs. Stanley J. Winkleman.

Let's Visit a Museum

This museum is in Detroit. It has art from all over the world.

Summing Up

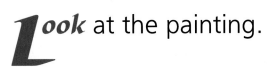

Look at the painting.

How many kinds of lines can you find?

The Detroit Institute of Art, Detroit, Michigan.

An Introduction to
Shape

Grant Wood. (American). *American Gothic.* 1930. Oil on Beaverboard. 74.3 × 62.4 cm. The Art Institute of Chicago, Illinois. ©1998 Estate of Grant Wood/Licensed by VAGA, New York, New York.

A shape is made with a line that traces the edge of the shape.

What shapes can you find in the painting?

Artist Profile

Grant Wood
1891–1942

Self-portrait

Grant Wood

- was an American artist.
- painted farm people.
- painted country scenes.

Lines Outline Shapes

Kenny Scharf. (American). *When Worlds Collide.* 1984. 10 ft, 2 inches × 17 feet, 5 inches. Courtesy of the Tony Shafrazi Gallery, New York, New York. © 1998 Kenny Scharf/Artists Rights Society (ARS), New York.

Trace with your finger the line around a shape you like in the painting.

Seeing like an artist

Trace a line around something near you. What shape did you make?

A line around the edge
of a **shape** is the **outline**.

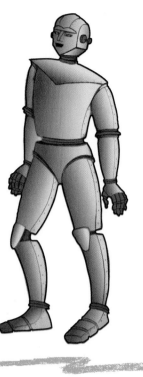

Create

What kinds of shapes do space creatures have?

Draw space creatures of your own.

Zoe Sommers. Age 6. *Space Creature*. Oil Pastel.

Geometric Shapes

Artist Unknown. (United States). *Album Quilt*. 1841–1844.
Pieced and appliquéd cotton fabric. 82 × 75 inches. National
Museum of American History, Smithsonian Institution,
Washington, DC.

Point to all the geometric shapes
on the quilt.

**Seeing like
an artist**

Look at your
clothes. Do you
see a ■, a ▲,
a ●, or a ▬?

Some shapes are **geometric shapes**.
Geometric shapes have names.

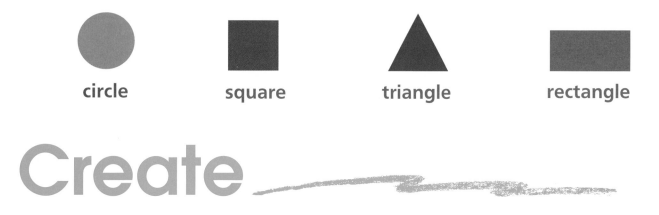

circle   square   triangle   rectangle

Create

What are your favorite geometric shapes?

Design a quilt with them.

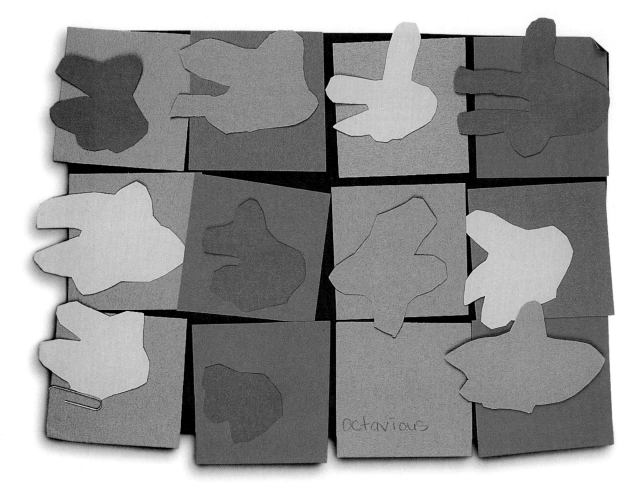

Octavious Baker. Age 5. *Shape Quilt.* Construction paper and glue.

Free-Form Shapes

David Wiesner. (American). *Free Fall.* Illustration.
Courtesy of Lothrop, Lee, and Shepard Books.

Point to the shapes in this painting that are not geometric shapes.

Seeing like an artist

Name a free-form shape you see. Trace the shape with your finger.

Artists use **free-form shapes** to show people, animals, and other things.

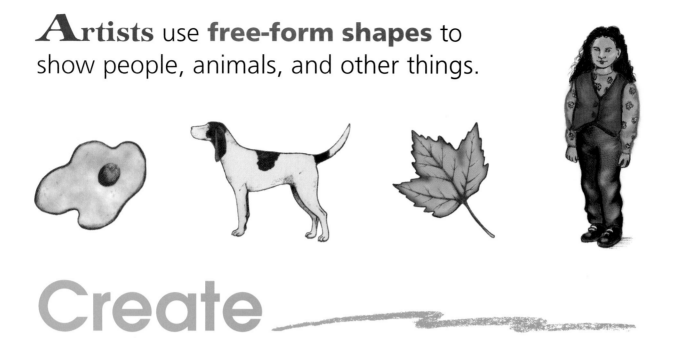

Create

Where do you see free-form shapes in nature?

Paint some free-form leaves.

Martin Rodriguez. Age 6. *Leaves.* Crayon and watercolor.

More About Shapes

Allan Crite. (American). *School's Out.* 1936. Oil on canvas.
$30\frac{1}{4} \times 36\frac{1}{8}$ inches. National Museum of American
Art, Washington, DC.

Find different shapes in this painting and name them.

Seeing like an artist
Name one thing you use in school. Is the shape geometric or free-form?

It's easy to find **geometric shapes** and **free-form shapes**. They're everywhere.

Create

How many geometric shapes and free-form shapes can you find?

Draw an inside-outside picture.

Madison Hendrix. Age 6. *Picture Frame.* Crayon.

Lesson 4

THE SHAPE OF ME

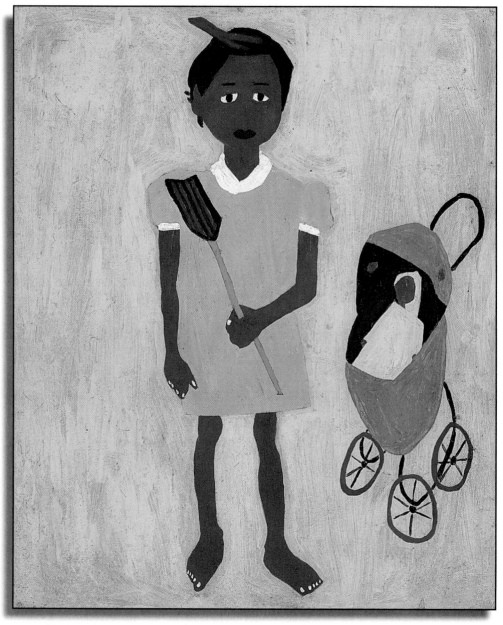

William H. Johnson. (American). *Li'l Sis*. 1944. Oil on paperboard. $26 \times 21\frac{1}{4}$ inches. National Museum of American Art, Washington, DC.

Artists use different shapes to show body parts. Name the body parts of the girl.

Seeing like an artist

Is your hand a free-form or a geometric shape?

Body parts are different shapes.
All body parts are **free-form shapes**.

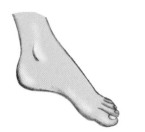

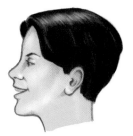

Create

How many free-form shapes does your body have?

Draw a big picture
of yourself.

Stephanie Gowdy. Age 6. *Myself*. Tempera and chalk.

THE SHAPE OF MY FAMILY

Ralph Earl. (American). *Mrs. Noah Smith and Her Family.* Oil on canvas.
$64 \times 85\frac{3}{4}$ inches. Metropolitan Museum of Art, New York, New York.
Gift of Edgar William and Bernice Chrysler Garbisch, 1964.

Point to the smallest person in the painting. Point to the biggest.

Seeing like an artist

Who is the tallest person in your room?

People are
all different sizes.
The **shapes**
used to draw people
are different sizes.

Create

How many different people sizes do you have in your family?

Draw a picture of them.

Allie Berlin. Age 5. *My Family.* Crayon.

Shape in Dance

AMAN International Folk Ensemble: "The Suite of Appalachian Music and Dance."

Jerry Duke creates dances. His dancers make lots of circles. His dancers sometimes work with puppets.

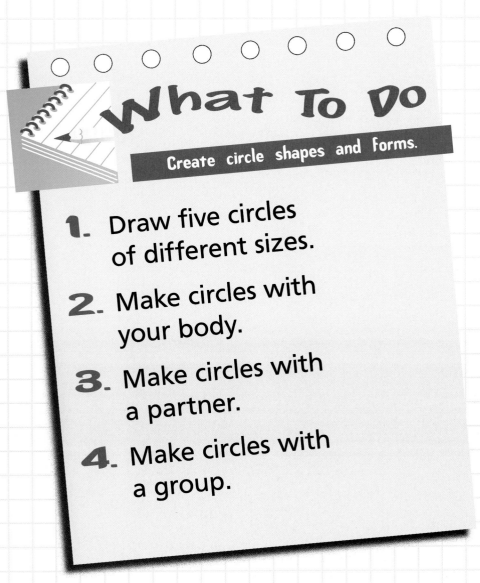

What To Do

Create circle shapes and forms.

1. Draw five circles of different sizes.

2. Make circles with your body.

3. Make circles with a partner.

4. Make circles with a group.

Extra Credit

**Practice the circles you made with your body.
Perform them for a group.**

Shape

Reviewing Main Ideas

Lines outline shapes.

There are geometric shapes and
free-form shapes.

Peter Bruegel the Elder. (Dutch). *Children's Games.* 1560. Oil on oakwood panel.
$46\frac{1}{2} \times 63\frac{3}{8}$ inches. Kuntshistariches Musems, Gemaeldegalerie, Vienna, Austria.
© Photograph by Erich Lessing, Art Resource, NY.

Jerry Pinkney began drawing when he was four years old. Now he makes beautiful pictures for books.

Summing Up

Find the shapes in the painting.

Can you name them?

Jerry Pinkney, book illustrator

An Introduction to

Henri Matisse. (French). *Purple Robe and Anemones.* 1937. Oil on canvas.
73.1 × 60.3 cm. The Baltimore Museum of Art: The Cone Collection, formed
by Dr. Claribel Cone and Miss Etta Cone of Baltimore, Maryland. © 1998
Succession H. Matisse, Paris/Artists Rights Society (ARS), New York.

Colors are everywhere.

What colors in the painting can you name?

Artist Profile

Henri Matisse
1869–1954

Henri Matisse

- was a great French artist.
- loved to paint bright colors.

A Garden of Colors

Peggy Flora Zalucha. (American). *Sprinkler Garden*
(diptych part 1). 1994. Transparent watercolor on paper.
36 × 52 inches. Private Collection.

Name the colors of the flowers
in this garden scene.

**Seeing like
an artist**

Look around
you. What colors
do you see?

Colors have names.

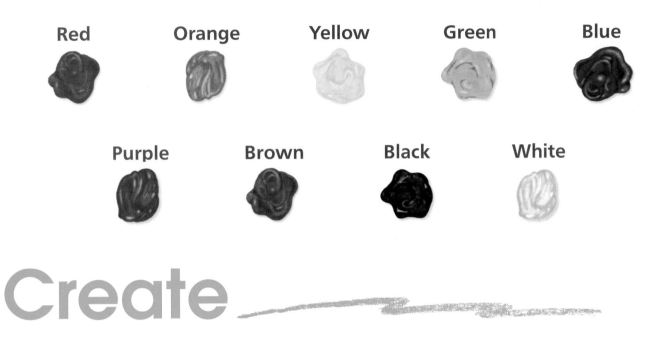

Red   Orange   Yellow   Green   Blue

Purple   Brown   Black   White

Create

What colors would you put in your garden?

Draw your own flower garden.

Lauren Knutti. Age 5. Pencil and crayon.

Identifying Colors

Claes Oldenburg. (Swedish). *Two Cheeseburgers With Everything (Dual Hamburgers)*. 1962. Burlap soaked in plaster, painted with enamel. $7 \times 14\frac{3}{4} \times 8\frac{5}{8}$ inches. The Museum of Modern Art, New York, New York. The Philip Johnson Fund. Photograph © 1998 The Museum of Modern Art, New York.

What kind of foods do you see in this artwork?

Seeing like an artist

Look around you. What objects do you see that are the color red?

Colors help us identify things.

Create

What do you like on your sandwiches?

Design a colorful sandwich **collage**.

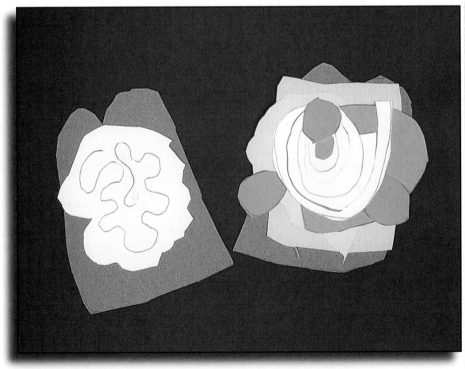

Riane Ramsey. Age 5. *My Yummy Lunch.* Paper Collage.

Painting with Colors

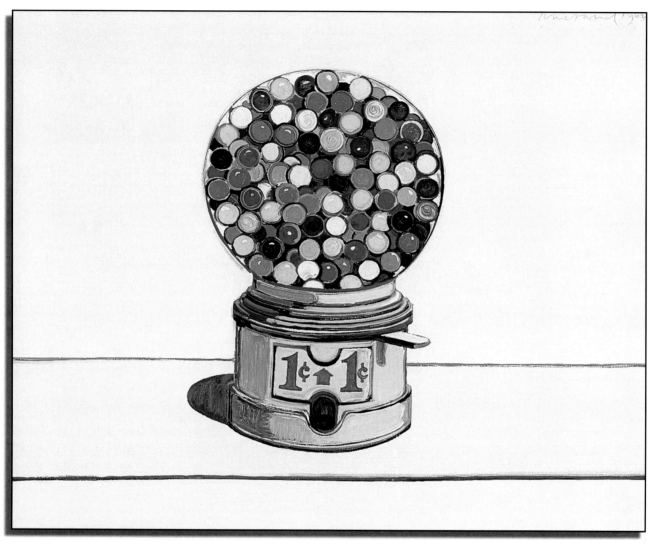

Wayne Thiebaud. (American). *Jawbreaker Machine.* 1963.
Oil on canvas. $26 \times 31\frac{1}{2}$ inches. Nelson-Atkins Museum of Art,
Kansas City, Missouri. Gift of Mr. and Mrs. Jack Glenn through
the Friends of Art.

Name the colors the artist used
in the **painting**.

Seeing like an artist

What colors
would you use
to paint your
favorite toy?

Artists use colors from real life
to make artwork look real.

Create

Where do you see your favorite colors?

Create a color collage.

Susan Morris. Age 5. *Blue*. Cut paper.

Bright and Dull Colors

Lynne Cherry. (American). *Great Kopack Tree.*
Illustration. © Lynne Cherry.

Where do you see bright colors
and dull colors in the painting?

Shapes stand out when you use **bright colors**. **Dull colors** make shapes hide.

Create

Name some places where you see many different colors.

Draw a rain forest scene.

Sam Crowley. Age 5. *Rainforest*. Crayons.

Color and Feelings

Artist unknown. (China). *Jar*. (Ming Dynasty, Hsuan-te mark and period 1426-35 from kilns at Ching-te Chen, Kiangsi Provence). Porcelain painted in underglaze blue. 19 inches high. Metropolitan Museum of Art, New York, New York.

How do you feel when you look at the dragon on this vase?

Seeing like an artist
Name a creature you have seen in a cartoon. What color is it?

Artists use **bright colors** to make us feel happy. **Dull colors** can make us feel sad or scared.

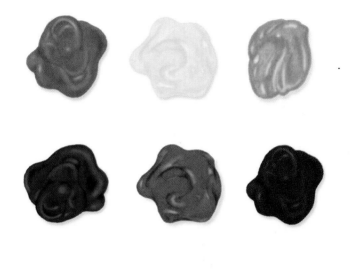

Create

How do different colors make you feel?

Paint a creature with colors you like.

Camron Nobles. Age 5. *Land of the Lost.* Watercolor and marker.

Light and Dark Colors

Graeme Base. (English). *Act II, Scene 1 "The Deep."* (From the book The Sign of the Sea Horse).

Point to a dark blue part of the painting. Now point to a light blue part.

Seeing like an artist

Look in a book. Find a picture that has light blue and dark blue.

Mixing colors with black or white makes them **darker** or **lighter**.

Create

What things in the sea have light and dark colors?

Create a sea picture with light and dark colors.

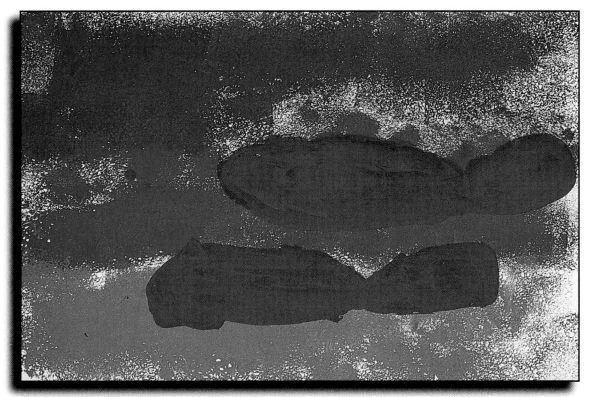

Jeanette Gutierrez. Age 5. *Fish*. Tempera.

Color in Music

Paul Salamunovich, Artistic Director for the Los Angeles Master Chorale.

Paul Salamunovich is a choral conductor.
He leads people in singing songs. He tells people when to sing fast or slow, soft or loud.

What To Do

Take a song you know and change the way you sing it.

1. Choose one song you know.

2. Sing the song in different ways.

3. Choose the color that best fits your song.

Extra Credit

Sing a new song.
Tell why the color best fits your song.

Color

Reviewing Main Ideas

Colors have names.

Colors help us identify things.

Marc Chagall. (Russian). *Paris Through the Window.* 1913. Oil on canvas. $53\frac{1}{2} \times 55\frac{1}{4}$ inches. Solomon R. Guggenheim Museum. New York, New York.

Let's Visit a Museum

This museum is in New York City. Part of the building is round.

Summing Up

*T**he** artist used many colors to create this painting.

Name the colors.

Solomon R. Guggenheim Museum. New York, New York.

An Introduction to
Space and Form

Alexander Calder. (American). *Calder's Circus*. 1926–31. Mixed Media. $54 \times 94\frac{1}{4} \times 95\frac{1}{4}$ inches. Collection of Whitney Museum of American Art, New York, New York. Purchase, with funds from a public fundraising campaign in May, 1982./©1998 Artists Rights Society (ARS), New York/ADAGP, Paris.

A form is a solid shape that takes up space.

What forms do you see in this artwork?

Artist Profile

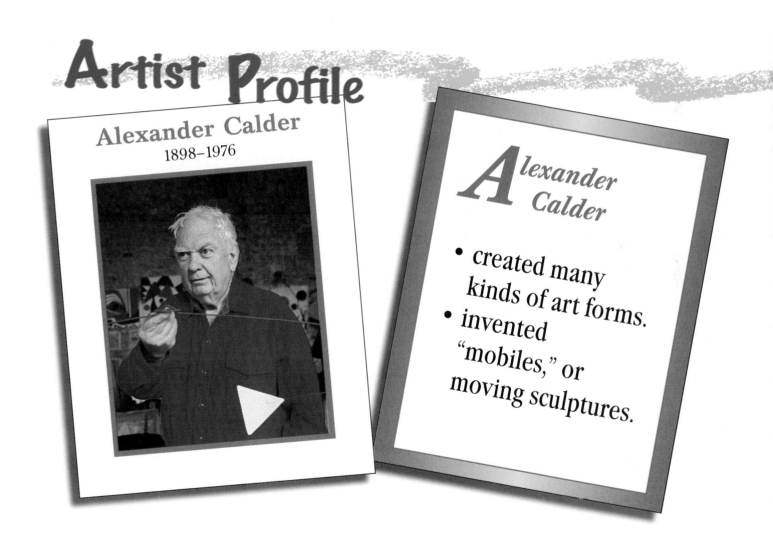

Alexander Calder
1898–1976

Alexander Calder

- created many kinds of art forms.
- invented "mobiles," or moving sculptures.

Space in Art

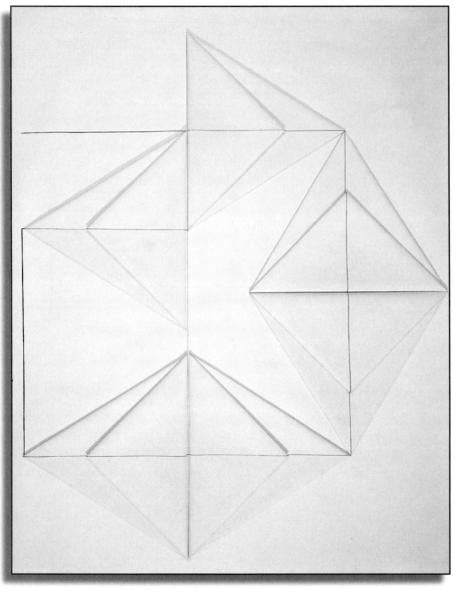

Dorothea Rockburne. (Canadian). *Sheba*. 1980. Gesso, oil, conte crayon, and glue on linen. $74 \times 59\frac{1}{2}$ inches. The National Museum of Women in the Arts, Washington, DC. Gift of Wallace and Wilhelmina Holladay. © 1998 Dorothea Rockburne. Artists Rights Society (ARS), New York.

Point to the empty areas around the shapes in this artwork.

Seeing like an artist

Do you see space around the clouds when you look in the sky?

The empty places around and between shapes are called **space**.

Create

How could you show space on paper?

Create a design using shapes.

Alberto Barojas. Age 5. *Shapes*. Crayons and cut paper.

Form

Felipa Trujillo. (American). *Man.* From the Girard
Foundation Collection, in the Museum of International
Folk Art, a unit of the Museum of New Mexico, Santa Fe,
New Mexico. Photographer: Michel Monteaux.

This form is a **sculpture**.
Describe what you think it
would look like from all sides.

Seeing like an artist

What are the
different sides of
a form you see in
your classroom?

A form is a **solid shape**.
You can look all around a form.

Create

What do you look like from different sides?

Create a form of you.

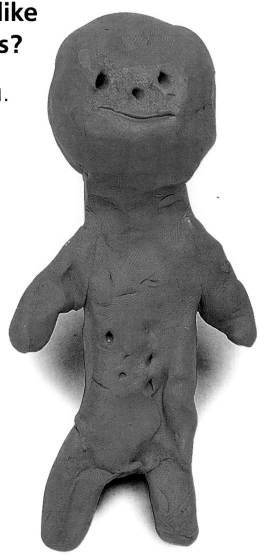

Natalie Norova. Age 5. *Happy Me.* Clay.

A Building Is a Form

Szopka. #81 Krakow, Poland. c.1960. Foil over cardboard. $50\frac{1}{4}$ inches high, Museum of International Folk Art, Santa Fe, New Mexico.

Name some of the different parts of this building.

Seeing like an artist

What parts of your school building do you see from outside?

A building is a **solid form**. You can walk around a building and see all the parts.

Create

What kinds of buildings have you seen?

Design your own building.

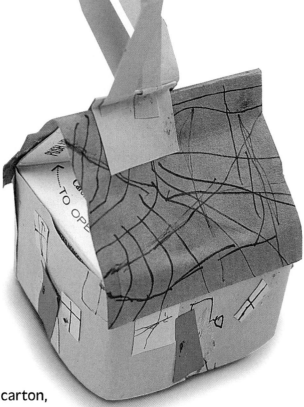

Isaac Justus. Age 5. *A Little House*. Milk carton, markers, and cut paper.

An Animal Is a Form

Artist unknown. (Egypt). *Ancient Egypt Hippo "William."* 1991–1786 B.C. Faience. 11 × 20 cm. Metropolitan Museum of Art, New York, New York. Gift of Edward S. Harkness, 1917.

What kind of animal form do you see in the picture?

Seeing like an artist

What other animals with four legs could be made as a sculpture?

An animal **sculpture** can be a **solid form**. You can walk around this animal form and see all four legs.

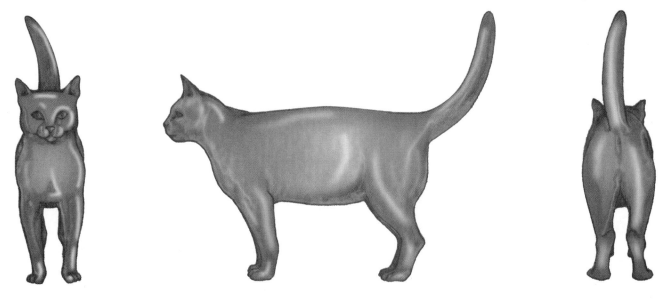

Create

What do your favorite animals look like?

Design an animal form.

Caitlin Cornwell. Age 5. *Slowie.* Clay and tempera.

Forms Can Have Designs

Artist unknown. (American). *Bottle Cap Giraffe.* 1966. Carved and painted wood, bottle caps, rubber, glass, animal hair, and fur. $72\frac{1}{2} \times 54 \times 17$ inches. National Museum of American Art, Smithsonian Institution, Washington, DC.

Name the things the artist used when designing this giraffe.

Seeing like an artist

Where else have you seen animals with designs?

Artists can turn different **forms** into make-believe creatures.

Create

What materials would you use to design your creature?

Create a make-believe creature.

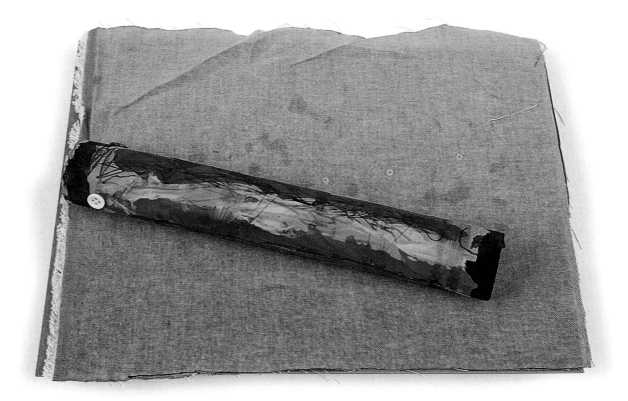

Nick Byers. Age 5. *Snakey.* Cardboard tube and tempera.

Forms Can Be Used

Artist unknown. (China). *Painted Storage Jar.* c. 2500 B.C. Clay, iron oxide, and magnesium pigments. 15 inches high × 16 inches in diameter. Kimbell Art Museum, Fort Worth, Texas.

How would you use the jar in this picture?

Seeing like an artist

Where do you see forms that are pretty and useful?

Jars and bowls are an **art form** that people look at and use.

Create

How could you design an artwork to use at home?

Create a pinch pot.

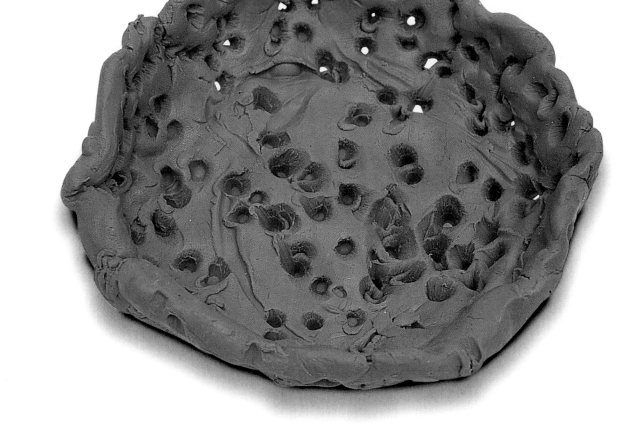

Liz Merckling. Age 5. *Pinched.* Clay.

Form in Theater

Sandy Spieler is the leader of a puppet and mask theater. She and other people are in a May Day parade. They bring giant puppets.

In the Heart of the Beast Puppet and Mask Theatre: Dragon puppet in May Day Parade and Festival.

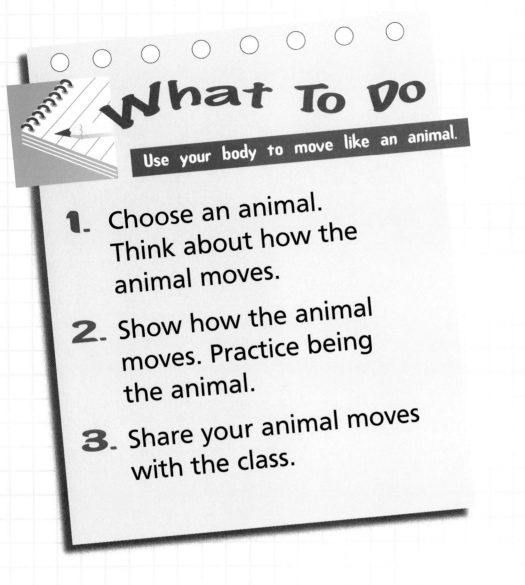

What To Do

Use your body to move like an animal.

1. Choose an animal. Think about how the animal moves.

2. Show how the animal moves. Practice being the animal.

3. Share your animal moves with the class.

Extra Credit ·

Make the sound a real animal makes. Ask others to move like that animal.

Space and Form

Reviewing Main Ideas

A form is a solid shape that takes up space.

You can see a form from all sides.

Artist Unknown. (Russian). *Russian Doll.* 1991. Wood with oil paint. 8 inches. Hudak private collection.

Summing Up

The space inside the form of the doll is filled with smalller dolls.

What kind of form is the doll?

Careers in Art

When Chris Down was a little boy, he liked to draw and build things. Now he designs new toys.

Chris Down, toy designer

An Introduction to

Texture

Harriet Powers. (American). *Bible Quilt, Detail: Dark Day of May 19, 1817. Pieced and appliquéd cotton embroidered with plain and metallic yarns.* Courtesy of the Museum of Fine Arts, Boston, Massachusetts. Bequest of Maxim Karolik.

Texture is the way something feels.

How do you think this quilt, or blanket, feels to the touch?

Artist Profile

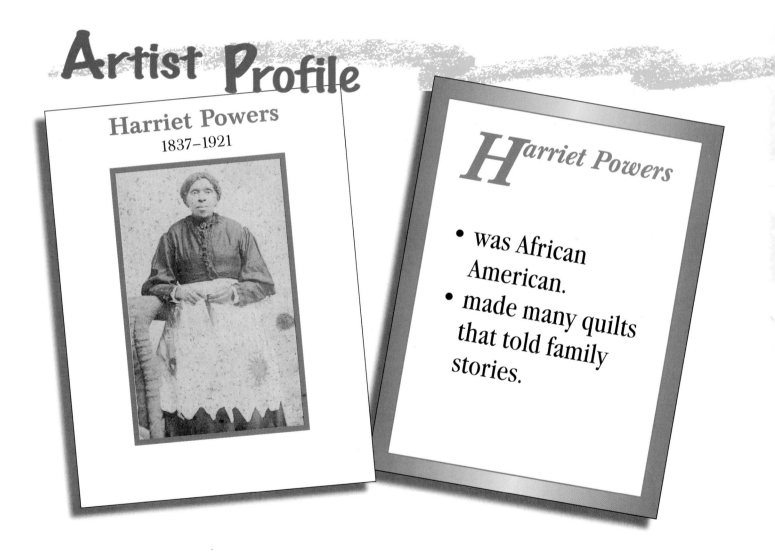

Harriet Powers
1837–1921

Harriet Powers

- was African American.
- made many quilts that told family stories.

Texture You Can Touch

Betty Parsons. (American). *Winged Frog.* 1978. Mixed-media wood construction. 27 × 20 inches. The National Museum of Women in the Arts, Washington, DC. Gift of Wallace and Wilhelmina Holladay.

This frog is made of wood. Point to the part of the frog that you think feels rough.

Seeing like an artist
Describe how textures in your classroom feel.

Something you can feel with your fingers is called **real texture**.

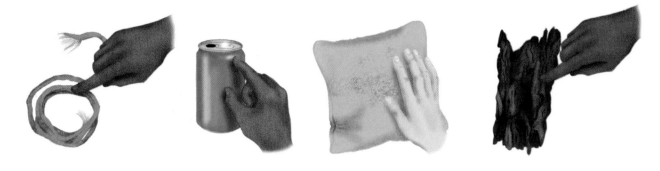

Create

How many different textures can you put in a **collage**?

Create a collage with textures.

Dillon. Age 6. *House and Yard.* Mixed media.

Texture You Can See

Gabriele Münter. (German). *Child with Ball.* c. 1916. Oil on canvas. $20\frac{1}{2} \times 17$ inches. The National Museum of Women in the Arts, Washington, DC. On loan from the Wallace and Wilhelmina Holladay Collection/© 1988. © 1996 Artists Rights Society (ARS), New York/VG Bild-Kunst, Bonn.

How do you think the child's hat would feel to touch?

Seeing like an artist

How could you draw the texture of something you see?

Texture you can see but cannot touch is **visual texture**.

Create

How can you show how different things feel?

Design a hat that has different textures.

David Belk. Age 5. *Top Hat*. Crayon.

Designing with Texture

Artist unknown. (Western Europe). *Hand Puppets.* Late nineteenth century. Painted wood. 16 inches high (on average). Museum of International Folk Art, Santa Fe, New Mexico.

Name the kinds of textures you see on the heads and bodies of these puppets.

Seeing like an artist

Tell about the textures of a puppet you have seen.

Cloth and yarn are **fibers**.
Fibers have different **textures**.

smooth

rough

bumpy

fuzzy

scratchy

Create

Where would you place different textures on a puppet?

Create a puppet with textures.

Jay Warden. Age 5. *Nojay.* Paper bag, buttons, and material.

Fiber Textures

Artist unknown. (United States). *Appalachian Basket.*
1988. 12 × 12 inches. Split Oak. Hudak Private Collection.

How do you think the basket shown here feels to the touch?

Wood, straw, and grass are **fibers**.
Many fibers are found in nature.

Create

What fibers would you use to make a basket of your own?

Weave a basket.

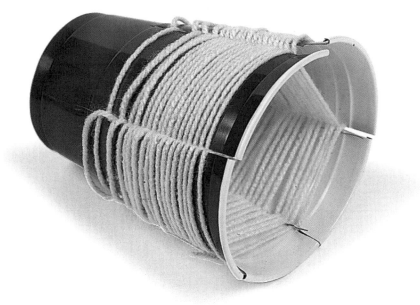

Julie Santana. Age 5. *Pretty*. Yarn and plastic cup.

Real Texture in Forms

Artist unknown. Ashanti people (Ghana). *Fish, Gold Weight*. Nineteenth–twentieth century. Bronze. $3\frac{1}{2}$ inches high. Metropolitan Museum of Art, New York, New York.

What do you think this fish would feel like if you could touch it?

Seeing like an artist

What kinds of lines would you use to make a clay tiger?

Tools or objects can be used to add **texture** to artwork. The texture that you can feel is called **real texture**.

Create

What objects would you use to show real texture?

Create a tile with real texture.

Thomas Harding. Age 5. *My Birthday Cake.* Clay, string, and beads.

Texture in Shapes

Elizabeth Valentine. (American). *Sampler.* c. 1935. Watercolor, graphite, and gouache on paper. $11\frac{3}{4} \times 8\frac{5}{8}$ inches. National Gallery of Art, Washington, DC. Index of American Design, © Board of trustees.

Point to the shapes this artist created with yarn on the cloth. This art is called **stitchery**.

Seeing like an artist

What shapes did the artist stitch in the picture?

Artists sew yarn to add **real texture** to artwork.

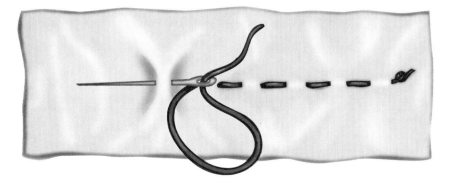

Create

What kinds of designs can you sew on cloth?

Sew your own design.

Kara Bloom. Age 5. *Pyramid.* Burlap and yarn.

Texture in Theater

Geri Keams, storyteller.

Geri Keams is "The Quillwork Girl." She is a storyteller. One story she tells is about a girl who sews porcupine quills on buckskin.

What To Do

Tell a story.

1. Listen to a story.

2. Talk about the story.

3. Role-play the story with others.

Extra Credit

Draw your favorite part of the story.

Texture

Reviewing Main Ideas

You feel real texture with your hand.

You see visual texture with your eyes.

Artist Unknown. (West African, Benin Kingdom). *Bronze Head for the Altars of the Obas.* Bronze. Nelson-Atkins Museum, Kansas City, Missouri.

Let's Visit a Museum

This museum is in Kansas City. It has art from all over the world.

Summing Up

This sculpture has real texture

How do you think it would feel?

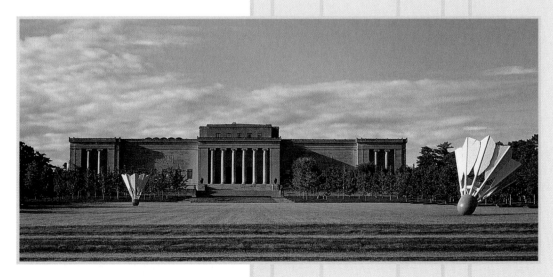

Nelson-Atkins Museum, Kansas City, Missouri.

An Introduction to

Rhythm, Balance, and Unity

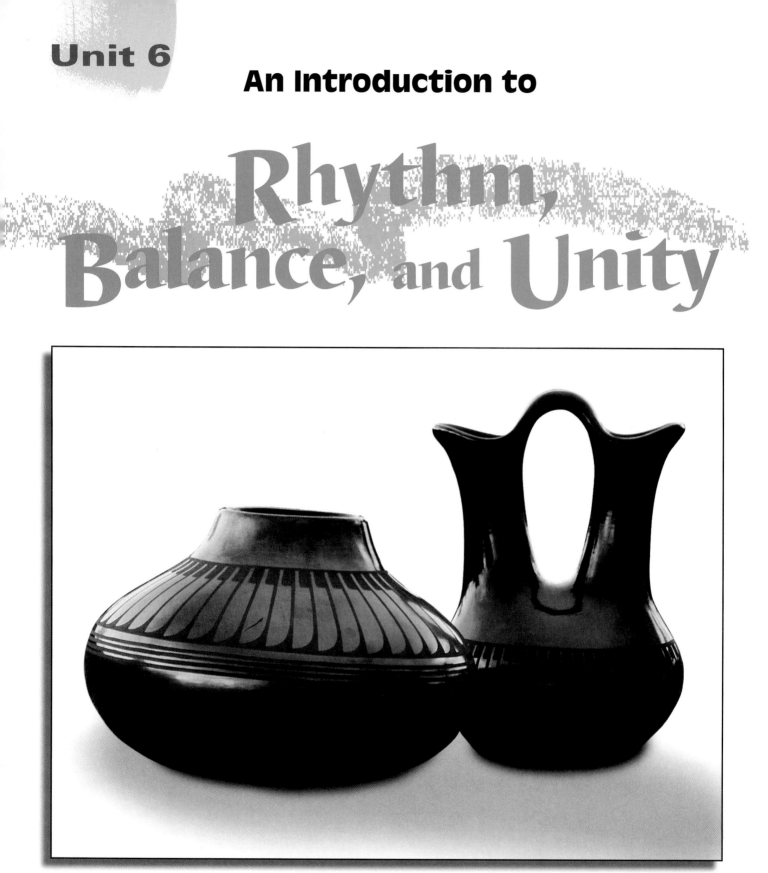

Maria Martínez. (American). *Two Black-on-Black Pots.*

An artist can repeat lines, shapes, or patterns in an artwork.

What has the artist repeated on the pottery?

Artist Profile

Maria Martínez
1887–1980

Maria Martínez

- was from New Mexico.
- was a Pueblo potter.
- Her husband decorated her pottery.

Balance

Chuck Close. (American). *Self Portrait/Close, Chuck.*
1987. Oil on canvas. 72 × 60 inches. Photograph courtesy
of Pace Wildenstein Gallery, New York, New York. Photo by
Bill Jacobson.

How can you tell that the face
of this man has even balance?

**Seeing like
an artist**
Study the face
of your teacher.
Tell why it is
balanced.

Fold a shape in half. When both halves are exactly the same, the shape has **even balance**.

Create

How does your face look in the mirror?

Draw it to show even balance.

Cecilia Lennox. Age 5. *Buttons*. Marker and buttons.

Even Balance with Animals

Artist unknown. (China). *Butterfly.* c. 1950. Cut paper.
$8\frac{1}{2} \times 15\frac{1}{8}$ inches. Museum of International Folk Art,
Santa Fe, New Mexico. From the Girard Foundation
Collection in the Museum of International Folk Art, a
unit of the Museum of New Mexico. Photographer:
Michel Monteaux.

One half of this butterfly looks
the same as the other half. Point
to the parts on each half.

Seeing like an artist

How many other
animals can you
name that have
even balance?

An animal has **even balance**. The left half and the right half of an animal are the same.

Create

What would a bug with even balance look like?

Create a make-believe bug.

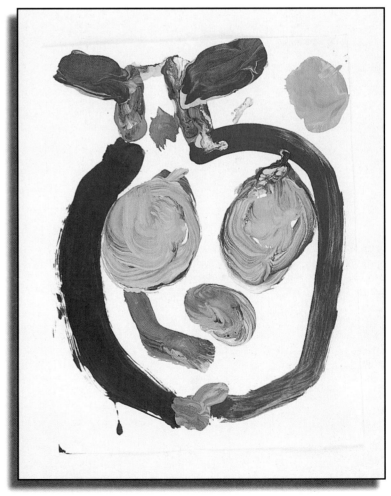

Karel Davis. Age 6. *Bug*. Tempera.

Pattern and Rhythm

Kuna Women. (Panama). *Mola: Group Project of Kuna Women.* Layered and cut fabric with stichery. Private collection. Photograph by ©Frank Fortune.

This artist uses shapes, lines, and colors. Find them.

Seeing like an artist

Find lines, shapes, and colors in your clothes that repeat.

Repeating a line, a **shape**, or a color in artwork creates a **visual rhythm**.

Create

How can you create a visual rhythm in an artwork?

Draw a parade of animals.

Caycee Creamer. Age 5. *Animal Parade*. Marker.

Rhythm and Movement

Jack Savitsky. (American). *Train in Coal Town.* 1968.
Oil on fiberboard. $31\frac{1}{4} \times 47\frac{3}{4}$ inches. National Museum of
American Art, Smithsonian Institution, Washington, DC.
Art Resource, New York.

What shapes did the artist
repeat in this painting?

Seeing like
an artist
What shapes
would you repeat
to show a car or
a boat moving?

Repeated shapes will create a sense
of **rhythm** and **movement**.

Create

How can you draw something to show movement?

Paint a moving train.

Travis Adkins. Age 5. *Train.* Oil pastel.

Rhythm and Printing

Artist unknown. (Kenya). *Printed Fabric from Bambalulu Handcraft Center.* 1993. Cotton with gold fabric ink. $2 \times 2\frac{1}{2}$ feet. Private Collection.

Find the animal that is repeated on this cloth. How do you think the artist repeated this shape?

Pressing a shape from one thing to another many times is called **printing**.

Create

What kinds of shapes would you find in a rain forest?

Print a rain forest shape.

Gabriele Mata. Age 5. *Rainforest Snake.* Tempera.

Rhythm Helps Make Unity

John Biggers. (American). *Shotguns, Fourth Ward.*
1987. Acrylic and oil on board. $41\frac{3}{4} \times 32$ inches.
Hampton University Museum, Hampton, Virginia.

What shapes are repeated in this artwork? Name them.

Seeing like an artist
What shapes do you see repeated in your school?

Repeated shapes and colors create
a feeling of **unity**, or belonging together.

Create

What kinds of shapes are repeated in your neighborhood?

Create a **mural** about your neighborhood.

Williamston Primary School. Ages 5–6. *All Through the Town.* Tempera.

Rhythm in Music

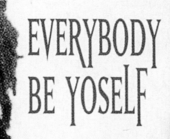

Chic Street Man, musician.

Chic Street Man sings and plays the guitar. He writes his own songs. His songs tell stories.

What To Do

Show the rhythm of a nursery rhyme.

1. Say a nursery rhyme.

2. Clap your hands to the nursery rhyme.

3. Stamp your feet to the nursery rhyme.

Extra Credit

Do a pantomime of the nursery rhyme.

Rhythm, Balance, and Unity

Reviewing Main Ideas

A shape has even balance when both halves are the same.

Repeating a line, a shape, or a color in art creates visual rhythm.

Repeated shapes and colors create a feeling of unity, or belonging together.

Berthe Morisot. (French). *The Sisters.* 1869. Oil on canvas. $20\frac{1}{2} \times 32$ inches. Gift of Mrs. Charles S. Carstairs, ©1996 Board of Trustees, National Gallery of Art, Washington, DC.

Careers in Art

Berthe Morisot lived a long time ago. She earned her living as an artist.

Summing Up

Morisot repeated lines, shapes, and colors to create rhythm in the painting.

What is the same on both sides of this picture?

Berthe Morisot, painter

Technique Tips

Drawing

Pencil

Thin lines.

Thick lines.

Crayon

Thin lines.

Thick lines.

Small dots.

Large dots.

Large spaces.

Marker

Use the tip.

Use the side of the tip.

Put on the cap.

Technique Tips

Oil Pastels

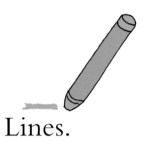

Lines.

Color in large spaces.

Blend colors.

Colored Chalk

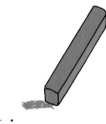

Lines.

Color in large spaces.

Blend colors.

Technique Tips

Painting

Taking Care of Your Paintbrush

Rinse and blot to change colors.
Clean your brush when you are done.

1. Rinse.

2. Wash with soap.

3. Rinse again and blot.

4. Shape.

5. Store.

More About...
Technique Tips

Tempera

Wipe your brush.

Mix on a palette.

Use a wide brush for large spaces.

Use a thin, pointed brush for details.

Technique Tips

Watercolor

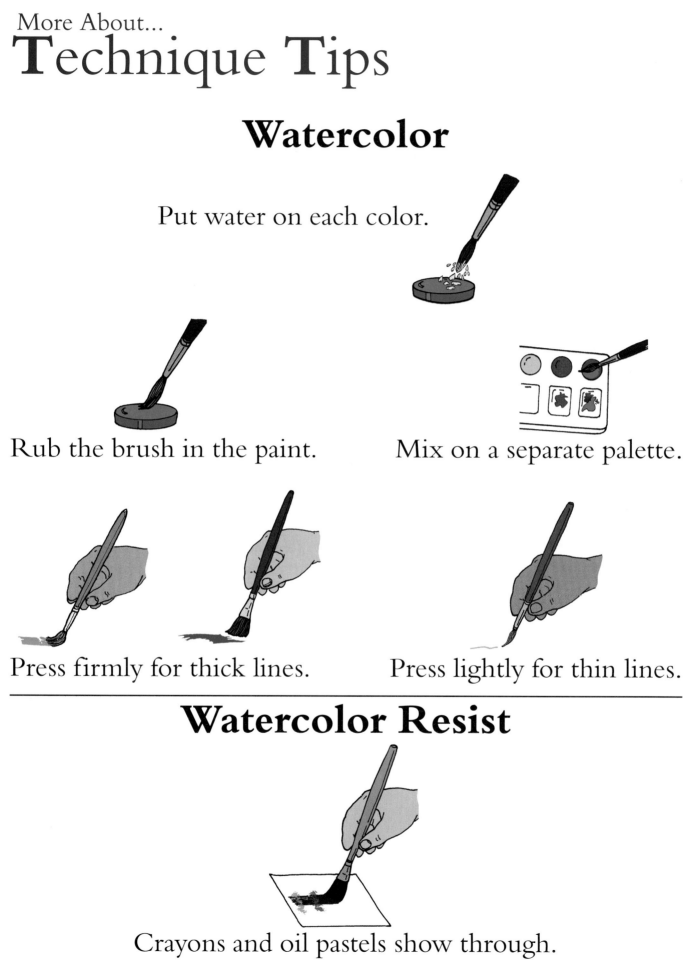

Put water on each color.

Rub the brush in the paint.

Mix on a separate palette.

Press firmly for thick lines.

Press lightly for thin lines.

Watercolor Resist

Crayons and oil pastels show through.

Technique Tips

Collage
Using Scissors

Hold scissors this way.

Always cut away from your body.

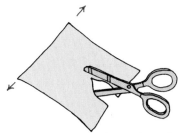

Have a friend stretch cloth as you cut.

Do the same with yarn.

Technique Tips

Using Glue

Use only a few glue dots on one paper.
Smooth with the tip of the glue bottle.

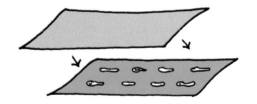

Press the papers together.

Clean the top and close the bottle.

Technique Tips

Arranging a Design

Tear shapes.

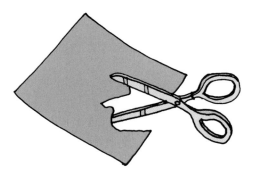

Cut shapes.

Use real objects.

1. Make a design.

Do you like the shapes and spaces?
Do you like the colors?
Do you like the textures?

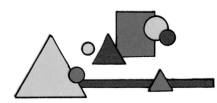

2. Glue the pieces in place.

Technique Tips

Printmaking

Making a Stamp Print

Paint the stamp.

Press the stamp onto paper and lift.

Sculpting

Working with Clay

Squeeze, pull, and shape to make clay soft.

Squeeze and pinch.

Pinch and pull.

Carving Clay

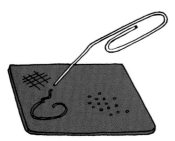

Use a pointed tool.

Technique Tips

Embroidery

Thread a needle.

Use a running stitch.

Technique Tips

Weaving

Making a Paper Loom

1. Fold paper in half.

2. Cut on folded edge.

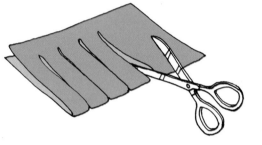

3. Don't cut to the other end.

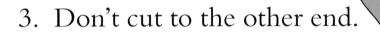

Weaving on a Paper Loom

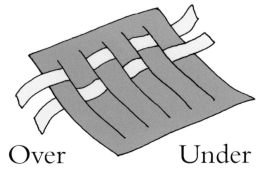

Over   Under

Grant Wood. (American). *American Gothic.* 1930. Oil on beaverboard. 73.3 × 62.4 cm.
The Art Institute of Chicago, Illinois. © 1998 Estate of Grant Wood/Licensed by VAGA, New York, NY.

More About...
Art Criticism

DESCRIBE

Who do you see?

What do you see?

ANALYZE

What colors do you see?

What shapes do you see?

Grant Wood. (American). *American Gothic.* 1930. Oil on beaverboard. 73.3 × 62.4 cm.
The Art Institute of Chicago, Illinois. © 1998 Estate of Grant Wood/Licensed by VAGA, New York, NY.

INTERPRET

What is happening in the painting?

DECIDE

Have you seen other artworks like this?

LOOK

Look at the painting.

Grant Wood. (American). *American Gothic.* 1930. Oil on beaverboard. 73.3 × 62.4 cm. The Art Institute of Chicago, Illinois. © 1998 Estate of Grant Wood/Licensed by VAGA, New York, NY.

LOOK AGAIN

Look at the painting?

What do you hear?

What do you think is in the house?

LOOK INSIDE

Look at the painting.

Pretend you are in the work of art.

What are you doing?

Grant Wood. (American). *American Gothic.* 1930. Oil on beaverboard.
73.3 × 62.4 cm. The Art Institute of Chicago, Illinois.
© 1998 Estate of Grant Wood/Licensed by VAGA, New York, NY.

LOOK OUTSIDE

Look at the painting.

What are the people thinking?

What do the people see?

What will you remember
about this work?

Artist unknown.
Yellow Horse. (*Chinese Horse*).
15,000–10,000 B.C. France.

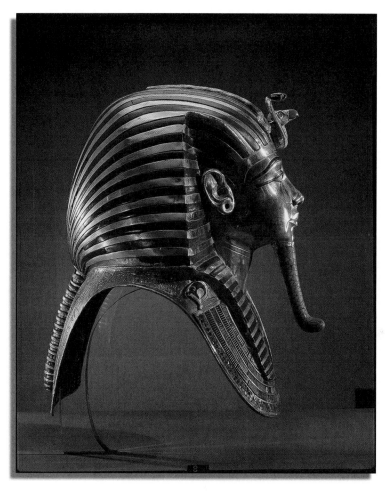

Artist unknown.
*Tutankhamen Mask
(side view).*
c. 1340 B.C. Egypt.

Leonardo da Vinci.
Mona Lisa. 1503. Italy.

Mary Cassatt.
Susan Comforting the Baby.
United States.

Subject Matter

Artists make art about many subjects. What subjects do you see here?

People

Mary Cassatt. (American). *Spring: Margot Standing in a Garden.* 1902. Oil on canvas. $26\frac{3}{4} \times 22\frac{3}{4}$ inches. The Metropolitan Museum of Art, NY. Bequest of Ruth Alms Bamard, 1982.

More About...
Subject Matter

Objects

Vincent van Gogh. (Dutch). *Irises.*
Oil on canvas. $29 \times 36\frac{1}{4}$ inches.
Metropolitan Museum of Art, New
York. Gift of Adele R. Levy, 1958.
Photograph by Malcom Varon.

Stories

Edward Hicks. (American). *Noah's
Ark.* Oil on canvas. $26\frac{5}{16} \times 30\frac{3}{8}$
inches. Philadelphia Museum of
Art: Bequest of Lisa Norris Elkins.

More About...
Subject Matter

Things Outside

Currier and Ives. (American).
A Ride to School. 5 × 8 inches.
The Metropolitan Museum of Art,
New York, New York.

Colors and Shapes

Joan Miró. (Spanish). *Women and
Bird in the Moonlight.* 1949.
The Tate Gallery, London, England.

More About...
Subject Matter

Everyday Life

Henri Matisse. *The Painter's Family.* 1911. The Hermitage Museum, St. Petersburg, Russia.

Things with a Deeper Meaning

Bookcover: Mary Emmerling's American Country Hearts. Photograph by Chris Mead. © by Chris Mead.

More About...
Seeing Lines

Most pictures have lines you already know.

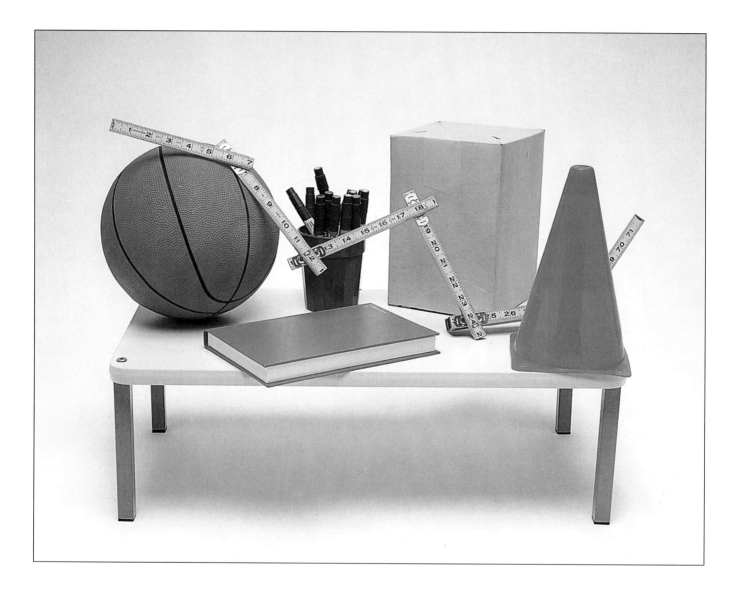

More About...
Seeing Lines

LOOK

Find these lines in the picture.

Straight

Curved

Zigzag

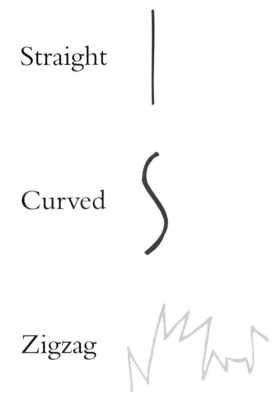

More About...
Seeing Shapes

Most pictures have shapes you already know.

More About...
Seeing Shapes

LOOK

Look for these shapes in the picture.

circle

square

rectangle

triangle

free-form

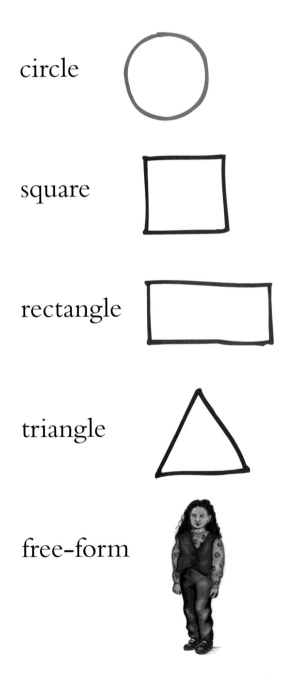

More About...
Seeing Size

What makes things look large or small?

More About...
Seeing Size

LOOK

Look at the picture.

Which horse is largest?

Which horse is smaller?

Which horse is smallest?

Visual Index

Artist unknown
Painted Storage Jar
2500–1700 B.C.
page 78

Artist unknown
Hippopotamus, "William"
1991–1786 B.C.
page 74

Artist unknown
Ravenna Apse Mosaic (detail)
100
page 22

Artist unknown
Jar
1426–1435
page 58

Katsushika Hokusai
Boy Juggling Shells
1760–1849
page 20

Ralph Earl
Mrs. Noah Smith and Her Family
c. 1780
page 42

Visual Index

Ito Jakuchu
Fukurojin, the God of Longevity and Wisdom
1790
page 18

Artist unknown
Album Quilt
1841–1844
page 34

Winslow Homer
Snap the Whip
1872
page 24

Artist unknown
Classic Serape Style Wearing Blanket
1875
page 14

W.H. Brown
Bareback Riders
1886
page 16

Artist unknown
Hand Puppets
Late nineteenth century
page 90

Visual Index

Artist unknown
Fish, Gold Weight
Nineteenth-twentieth century
page 94

Artist unknown
Appalachian Basket
1980s
page 92

Kuna Women
Mola
Twentieth century
page 108

Artist unknown
Printed Fabric from Bambalulu
1993
page 112

Felipa Trujillo
Man
Early 1900s
page 70

Gabriele Münter
Child with Ball
1916
page 88

Visual Index

Elizabeth Valentine
Sampler
1936
page 96

Allan Crite
School's Out
1936
page 38

William H. Johnson
Li'l Sis
1944
page 40

Artist unknown
Butterfly
1950
page 106

Artist unknown
Szopka
1960
page 72

Claes Oldenburg
Two Cheeseburgers With Everything (Dual Hamburgers)
1962
page 52

Visual Index

Wayne Thiebaud
Jawbreaker Machine
1963
page 54

Artist unknown
Bottle Cap Giraffe
1966
page 76

Jack Savitsky
Train in Coal Town
1968
page 110

Betty Parsons
Winged Frog
1978
page 86

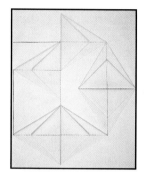

Dorothea Rockbourne
Sheba
1980
page 68

Peggy Flora Zalucha
Sprinkler Garden
1994
page 50

Visual Index

Kenny Scharf
When Worlds Collide
1984
page 32

John Biggers
*Shotguns,
Fourth Ward*
1987
page 114

Chuck Close
Self Portrait
1987
page 104

David Wiesner
Free Fall
1988
page 36

Lynne Cherry
The Great Kapok Tree
1990
page 56

Graeme Base
Act II, Scene I "The Deep"
1992
page 60

Glossary

art form

A type of art.

brown

black

circle

○

blue

collage

Bits and pieces of things glued onto paper.

curved line

bright color

darker

broken line

Glossary

dull color

even balance

Both halves are equal. Left side and right side are the same.

fiber

A material used to make baskets and cloth. Grass, yarn, and straw are kinds of fibers.

form

free-form shape

geometric shapes

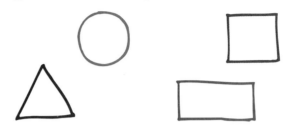

green

lighter

line

Glossary

movement

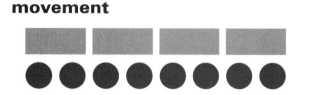

printing

Pressing a shape from one thing to another many times.

mural

A painting done on a wall.

purple

orange

real texture

Texture you can feel.

rectangle

outline

red

painting

An art form using paint on a flat surface.

Glossary

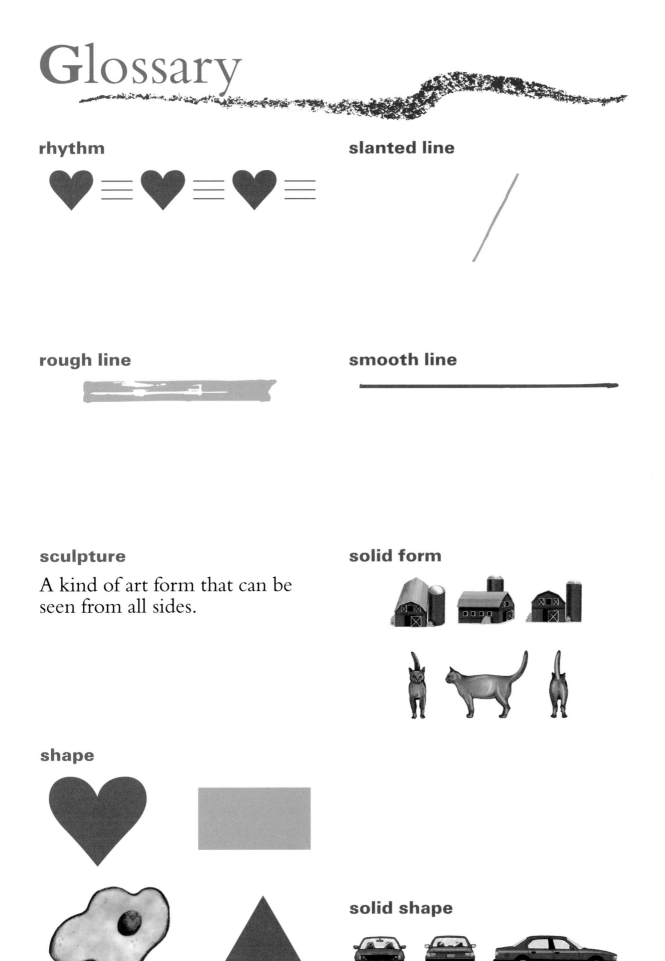

rhythm

slanted line

rough line

smooth line

sculpture

A kind of art form that can be seen from all sides.

solid form

shape

solid shape

Glossary

space

texture

How something feels.

square

thick line

stitchery

Art made with yarn on cloth.

thin line

straight line

triangle

Glossary

unity

A feeling of belonging together.

visual rhythm

visual texture

Texture you can see, but cannot touch.

white

yellow

Index

Index

Index